THE MIND CURE:

Christian D. Larson

COPYRIGHT 2018
Premium Classic Books

Premiumclassicbooks@gmail.com

CONTENTS

THE MIND CURE: 1
HOW TO OVERCOME NERVOUSNESS AND FEAR 1
   ABOUT THIS BOOK.. 1
     1. THE CURE OF NERVOUSNESS 3
     2. GOOD HEALTH FOR THE MIND................................. 38
     3. THE CURE OF DESPONDENCY.................................. 49
     4. THE PREVENTION OF MENTAL DEPRESSION 68
     5. HOW TO REMOVE FEAR 74

THE MIND CURE:
HOW TO OVERCOME NERVOUSNESS AND FEAR

ABOUT THIS BOOK

If our mind works soundly, we are in good shape. However, working soundly does not refer to a physical think. It refers to our thoughts, our attitudes, and the kind of things we feed our mind.

In this book, Larson teaches us how the health of the mind is fundamental for life. With a series of "mind cures" he gives us advice to eliminate nervousness, despondency, fear and depression.

On Nervousness "The fact is, if nervousness were completely removed from the race more than half of the physical ills, and nearly all the mental ills, would be removed. The strength and endurance of the body would be increased remarkably, and the capacity of the mind would in most instances be practically doubled."

On curing despondency: "Recent discoveries in psychology have revealed the fact that no mental talent or faculty can grow to any satisfaction unless the mind realizes an abundance of brightness and joy."

On fear: "SO long as there is a tendency to fear it is not possible for any mind to do its best, and as it is absolutely necessary for every mind to do its best in order to live the life of peace, health, freedom, and attainment, we must proceed to remove fear completely."

1. The Cure of Nervousness

IT IS a well-known fact that a considerable majority of the people in this country are addicted more or less to nervousness in one or more of its many forms; and as nervousness is the direct cause of all mental ills, and the indirect cause of a great many physical ills, organic as well as functional, there are few things that would be more important than that of finding a method through which health for the nerves could be secured. How to cure this malady has long been a problem. Medicine as a rule avails but little, and the various forms of other therapeutic systems reach but a limited number. It is therefore that the discovery of a remedy that could reach all cases, or nearly all cases, would easily be considered one of the most remarkable discoveries of the age. We may safely state that when people learn to keep the nervous system in perfect order there will be very few cases of insanity, if any, and physical diseases will be reduced at least one half. In addition to this, the power and capacity of mind will be increased to a very great degree. The majority of the fine minds in the world fail to do all they are capable of doing, because their talents are interfered with by nervous troubles of some kind, and these troubles not only tend to reduce the amount of mental energy, but also confuse the intellect and almost invariably misdirect the imagination. There is scarcely a mind living of exceptional ability or genius that is not addicted to nervousness of some form, and that any mind can do its best under such conditions is impossible.

The fact is, if nervousness were completely removed from the race more than half of the physical ills, and nearly all the mental ills, would be removed. The strength and endurance of the body would be increased remarkably, and the capacity of the mind would in most instances be practically doubled. That a perfect remedy for nervousness would therefore prove a great boon, to say the least, is evident; and a remedy has been found that fulfills all the requirements, because from its very nature it simply cannot fail. This remedy will give health to the nerves in every case where it is used, and it is so simple that all who will apply it can do so successfully.

That this remedy will remove nervousness in every instance may seem impossible, but when we examine the nature of the remedy we find that its never-failing effectiveness lies in its power to remove the remote cause of what may be termed the immediate cause of this ailment. That condition of the system that we call nervousness comes from discord in the nerve fluid, or what may be called confused vibrations in the electro-magnetic energies of the body. This is the immediate cause; but back of this cause there is a remote cause ; that is, that condition that originally produces the confused vibrations in those energies.

The nerve fluid we speak of may be termed human electricity, as its nature and actions correspond exactly with electrical currents, though, of course, it is much finer in quality than ordinary electricity. The human brain may accordingly be termed a dynamo, because those fine currents are generated there; and the nerves may be termed the wires that carry this fluid or electricity to every part of the body.

The functions of this nerve fluid are many. Every thought, state, condition or action produced in the mind is carried all through the body, over these nerves or wires, by the force of this fluid, and in return everything that is taking place throughout the system is conveyed to the brain by the same process. The nervous system is therefore a human telegraph system through which the mind is constantly kept informed concerning the events of its own world, and constantly giving directions with regard to what is to be done in every part of its world; and we can readily understand how false news or information can be transmitted, and how urgent news can be delayed in its passage, should these finer electrical currents be disturbed.

When a person is suffering from nervousness he is frequently deluded concerning the conditions of his system, the reason being that he is getting false news because the telegraph system is not in perfect order. In like manner, such a person may fail to get the exact facts concerning his conditions. There may be conditions brewing in his system of which he is not aware, because the news is lost on the way.

The same state of affairs, however, is frequently brought about by drugs. When you take drugs to stop pain, you do not remove the pain; you simply deaden the nerves so that the sensation or news of the pain cannot be carried to the brain. Occasionally such a process may be permissible, but if we interfere too much with the news-carrying function of the nervous system we will cripple it to such an extent that most of the sensations received will be false or magnified. When people imagine that they have ills that do not exist in their systems a crippled or perverted nervous system is generally the cause. They are getting false news about their own conditions, and they think it is true because it seems so real. Not everything is true, however, that seems real. The fact is that the more disturbance and perversion there is in the nervous system, the more real will also its false impressions appear to be; and the reason is that a disturbed nervous system is abnormally sensitive.

ANOTHER function of the nervous system is to transmit creative energy to every part of the body. Every cell in the system is constructed or repaired by creative energy, and this energy is conveyed by the nerve that enters the locality of that cell; consequently when the nervous system is out of order the process of repair, or cell construction, will be retarded in many places. When this process is interfered with, or the normal activities of the process are disturbed, the system will not only be left in bad repair, but false growths may be produced. When the creative forces are disturbed or misdirected in any part of the system they cannot continue in normal cell construction, but will in many instances begin to produce false cell construction. In this manner tumors, cancers, goiters, cataracts and all sorts of unnatural growths may originate.

And in this connection we should remember that practically all abnormal growths in the human system can be traced back to nervous conditions of some form. Perfect health for the nerves, therefore, if maintained all through life, would absolutely prevent all such unnatural growths in the human system. When the creative energies of the system continue in their normal activities no unnatural growth can possibly be formed, and to keep those energies in their normal state of action the nervous system must be in order; that is, every nerve must be in good health.

To go into details and outline fully the various effects that follow the actions of the nerve fluid would lead us into every phase of physiological psychology, and volumes would be required. It is not our purpose, however, to present a full treatise on this vast subject in this connection, but simply to present in the briefest manner possible the practical application of an effective remedy for the nerves. The various effects of the nerve fluid in all its functions will be right when the cause is right; and the cause is right when the vibrations of the electricity of the body are normal. To produce and maintain such normal vibrations must therefore be our purpose.

It has been stated that confusion among the vibrations of the nerve forces is the immediate cause of nervousness, and also that this force is generated in the brain; therefore, to find the cause of this confusion we must go to the brain, or rather to the mind. When we analyze the mind we find that every mental attitude produces a corresponding action in the brain and modifies to a degree the forces that are generated in the brain. As the brain is the dynamo generating nerve forces, or the electrical forces of the nervous system, it is evident that a disturbed mental state producing a corresponding action in the brain will confuse the vibrations of the forces generated in the brain during that particular state of mind.

To remove every confused attitude or disturbed state from the mind would, therefore, seem to be the perfect remedy; but this would constitute complete prevention, and not necessarily a remedy for effective use when actual nervousness was present. To prevent all nervousness one must become master over his thoughts and feelings and learn to create only those mental states that have a harmonious and wholesome effect upon the body; but this requires a thorough understanding of metaphysics, and also considerable time. In fact, it would necessarily be a steady growth. Besides, many of the disturbing mental states are in the subconscious, and cannot be removed until the entire mentality is renewed. To renew and perfect the subconscious as well as the conscious mind, should be the constant purpose of every person; but while he is changing his mind, his thought and his life, he must have some method to emancipate himself from those conditions, the adverse causes of which have not been removed.

Though we may be working for complete prevention, still while this work remains incomplete we need quick and ready remedies to remove the results of our mistakes, past or present. If we continue to work for complete prevention we will soon arrive at a place where our mistakes will be reduced to a minimum; but until we reach that state we must have remedies or methods that will remove the mistakes at once, so that no other ill effect may follow.

Then, again, there are thousands that have not the power to remain undisturbed in the midst of the world's confusion. They are constantly meeting discord, and need help present help to prevent such discord from producing detrimental effects. We therefore need effective remedies for the present, as well as a system of thinking and living through which we may gradually provide complete prevention.

WHEN we analyze the various conditions that disturb the nerves, we find that a disturbed state of mind is the remote cause, therefore peaceful states of mind must be the remedy. Disturbed states of mind will disturb the electric energies generated in the brain, and as these energies follow the nerves all through the system, the entire system will be in discord accordingly. On the other hand, peaceful states of mind will cause the electric energies generated in the brain to become calm, serene and harmonious, and as those energies are, so will be the entire nervous system. When we create only peaceful states of mind there will be no discord whatever in the system, and when discord disappears nervousness will also disappear.

When disturbed mental states have already been produced, they can be counteracted before they enter the nervous system, and their undesirable effects avoided. The process is simple, and may be applied effectually by anyone. In the first place, life and thought should be made as calm, serene and peaceful as possible; and, secondly, every cause of disturbance or nervousness, either acute or chronic, conscious or subconscious, should be removed by cultivating serenity and peace. While the nerve force is still in the brain you can modify its vibrations by changing the actions in the mind, but after this force has entered the spinal cord it will continue in its original vibrations until it has permeated the system. This force, therefore, must be acted upon before it enters the spinal cord, and since it responds readily to every action of mind, a complete change can be made if produced in the proper place.

To reach the energies of the brain directly, the mind should act upon the brain center, a point exactly midway between the opening of the ears. Draw an imaginary line from ear to ear through your brain, and divide that line in the center. At this point you will find the region of the brain center. In the region of the brain center the energy or nerve force that has been generated in the brain is transferred to the spinal cord, from whence it goes to every part of the system.

To change the vibrations of this force, therefore, before it enters the spinal cord, the mind must act upon the brain center, and must produce through that action the very condition that is desired in the nervous system as a whole. That state of mind that is impressed upon the brain center will cause all the nerve forces coming from the brain to be identical with the mental state itself, both in nature and action, therefore to impress upon the brain center a mental state of perfect harmony, calmness and poise, will cause the nerve force as it proceeds from the brain to become calm, harmonious and poised, and will accordingly convey calmness, harmony and poise to every part of the system.

When these calm nerve currents begin to pass through the system, every form of nervousness will begin to disappear, and relief will be felt at once. All weak actions of the heart will also cease and normal action be secured, because all heart troubles, practically, come from disturbances in the nervous system. To concentrate upon the brain center in the attitude of peace will cause the heart to become normal in its actions in a few moments, and if this method is employed several times every day for five or ten minutes, what is usually spoken of as heart disease will disappear without giving the least thought or attention to the heart itself.

To apply this method perfectly, turn your attention upon the brain center and concentrate gently upon this point while you are thinking calmly but deeply of poise, peace, serenity and harmony. Try to feel at the time that everything at the brain center is still, perfectly still ; that all is quiet, easy and at rest. And here we should remember that while this method is being employed we should not think of mind or body in the least, but all thought should be directed upon that peaceful state that we imagine is being produced at the brain center. If you can focus your whole attention upon the brain center at the time and feel that all the energies of mind and brain are moving gently toward the brain center, you are going to realize perfect harmony throughout your system, even in a few seconds. This peaceful state of mind will soon penetrate the entire region of the brain center, and all the energies that are passing from the brain to the spinal cord, and thence to the nervous system, will change and become calm and serene, as that condition is at the brain center through which those energies always pass. And as these are the only energies that act directly through the nervous system, all nervousness must disappear when those energies themselves become serene.

When this method is being applied it is best to be comfortably seated, or better still, to lie down with the mind and body relaxed, eyes closed, and all attention withdrawn from outer things. Then have but one purpose in view to penetrate the brain center with a mental life of absolute peace and calm. The more quietly and the more easily you go about this practice, the better you will succeed ; and to try to draw gently the finer mental forces toward the brain center as you think of the finer forces of your , mind, will aid remarkably in producing immediate results. It is well to breathe deeply, but gently, during the exercise, which may be continued for five or ten minutes, and repeated several times every day.

To combine physical breathing with this exercise, in any particular manner, will be found very helpful, and to this end proceed as follows:

While you inhale physically, try to draw the finer forces of mind and brain toward the brain center, and while you exhale physically, try to feel that those finer forces are moving with calmness and peace down through your body toward the feet. To combine physical breathing with what might be called inhalation and exhalation of the finer forces of the mind will, when carried out effectually, be found to be a method of incalculable value in all conditions of nervousness or mental disturbance. Every one, therefore, will find it profitable to practice this method until it can be carried out to perfection. When results begin to appear, an inner comfort will be felt that is delightful, and every nerve in the system will be quiet.

In this connection it is well to remember that the quiet nerve is the only nerve that is doing its work properly. Whenever you feel excited, agitated or disturbed, apply this method and immediately harmony will be restored, thus preventing both ills and mistakes. It will compose the system, restore the heart to its normal action, and give the creative energies that perfect poise that is so necessary to the keeping of the system in purity and repair. This method will also remove weariness and the tired feeling, because both mind and body are invariably recharged with energy when they are placed in perfect poise. When this method is employed daily and properly nervousness in every form will disappear, perfect health for the nerves will be secured, and the system will be placed in a higher degree of harmony a state that is most valuable in the promotion of physical or mental development.

To try to feel the finer essence or life of mind while concentrating in poise upon the brain center is very important, because when the finer life is felt the subconscious will be impressed; and when perfect peace is conveyed to the subconscious the good work is done. When the subconscious becomes calm and serene in all its actions every atom in the system will work in perfect harmony, and every action, no matter how rapid or how strong, will be absolutely calm and serene, important essential in the cure of nervousness is to remove the tendency to think or act unconsciously. Unconscious action that is, doing one thing while thinking about something else will produce a divided attention, and a divided attention leads to a decrease in the power of self-control. So long as the attitude of self-possession and self-control is perfect, nervousness will be impossible, but the moment the mind begins to lose its hold upon the various functions of the system, nervousness will begin.

What is called nervousness is nothing but confused action among the nerve energies, and as the mind is the original cause of every action that takes place in the human system, confused action anywhere in the system must come originally from confused mental action. The fundamental cause of confused mental action is divided attention, and divided attention comes from having several things on the mind at once.

One thing at a time should be the law. You may have a thousand duties to perform every day, but give direct attention to only one at a time. Train yourself to do this, and you will be absolutely free from nervousness all your life. A breakdown in the nervous system does not come from overwork, but from the scattering of your forces, and it is only through the dividing of your attention that your forces can be scattered. The dividing of attention, however, may be produced in a number of ways. To try to do too many things at once is one cause; living a complex life is another cause; though the principal cause is usually found in the reckless use of the imagination.

The majority do not know how to apply the imagination constructively, and therefore its actions are, as a rule, helter-skelter. The result is confused mental action, to be followed later by confused actions among the nerve forces. The same is true in all forms of life and thought where imagination is carried off, so to speak, into all sorts of abnormal states through excitement or various forms of mental intoxication. Mental confusion is the result, and when the forces of the mind are going helter-skelter the forces of the nerves will do the same, because the nervous system is directly connected with the brain in general, as with every individual action that takes place in the brain.

When the energy of the system runs low every function of body or mind, including the imagination, is crippled to a degree in its effort to continue normal actions. The result is abnormal or confused action, which may be followed by sickness of some kind, or by a nervous breakdown; but the original cause of a lack of energy in the system is not always physical. Physical dissipation, burning the candle at both ends, will reduce the energy of the body; and there is also such a thing as mental dissipation, some of the chief elements of which are anger, worry, excitement, mental depression, despondency, discouragement, reckless thinking and reckless imagination. Energy may therefore be wasted, both physically and mentally, but every action of waste comes originally from the mind, because the body can do nothing unless the mind originates the action. To remove the cause of nervousness, there are two factors to be considered. First, the vital energy of the system must be kept full and strong at all times. When vitality is insufficient, normal action becomes impossible. To cease normal action is to begin abnormal action.

Abnormal action leads to confused action, and confused action leads to nervousness. Second, mental disorder in all its forms must be removed completely; and this is accomplished by removing the habit of dividing attention. In brief, to remove the cause of nervousness, train yourself to give your whole attention now to whatever you may be thinking of or doing now, and so think and live that your system will be brimful of energy at all times. When you are constantly full of vital energy, and are constantly using your energy in the actions of harmony, poise and self-possession, you will never be nervous. Abundance of power in all your actions, and perfect poise in all your actions these are the two secrets.

TO secure abundance of power, you need not generate more than you are generating now. All that is necessary is to prevent what you are generating from being wasted. In brief, learn to use all your present energy so that all waste may be avoided completely. The power that is wasted is lost, but the power that is used produces increase. The power we use today will reappear in the system tomorrow, because everything that is properly used is like a seed sown in rich soil; it will reproduce itself, and will not only reappear with the original amount, but with more.

The first essential in the proper use of the power we possess is to have some definite purpose in view for every thought and action, and to give that purpose our undivided attention. When we think, we should think with a purpose, and should think of only one thing at a time. In that way all the power of our thought is put to work, and none of it is wasted. In this connection it is well to remember, and to repeat again, that weariness comes from the waste of power; never from power that is put to work. Power that is put to work reproduces itself, therefore no loss of power can follow ; and it is only when power is lost that weariness can be felt in the system.

When you work, do not think of the next step or try to plan for the next step while the work of the first is being finished. Take special moments for laying new plans. In this way you will not only work out the best plans, but you will avoid dividing your attention or confusing your mind. Do not let your head run faster than your feet; and do not live mentally in the future while you are working in the present. Where the body lives, the mind should live also, and the energies of both should work together in building up the life of the present moment.

When you read, do not try to read the second paragraph before you are through with the first, and do not skim over an article with a view of getting the substance out of it in one-tenth of the time it takes to read it. The habit of skimming over things is one of the worst mental habits in the world, and should be eliminated completely. We may think we gain time by skimming over things, but we lose energy and power, as well as mental brilliancy, and in the end it is all loss and no gain.

In your living, avoid the same mistake. Do not try to get all there is in life by hurrying through life. The majority, however, are addicted to this habit, but it leads directly to nervousness, and is the direct cause of more than ninety per cent of the nervous breakdowns that are produced. In the meantime, this same habit brings much destruction, depression and unhappiness. Learn to live in the present. Plan for the future during special moments selected for that purpose, but refuse absolutely to live in the future. Refuse to do in your mind today what you expect to do in the reality tomorrow. Thousands have this habit. In consequence their minds are nearly always confused, while they scatter their forces continually. If you are going to take a journey tomorrow, make your plans today, but do not take that journey a score of times in your mind today; or, if you are going to undertake something special tomorrow, get good and ready today, but do not mentally pass through the details of that work today.

Get ready the bricks for the building of tomorrow, but do not lay the bricks in your mind today. Never do with your mind today what you are to do with your hands tomorrow. Do not live over in your mind in the present the experiences you passed through in the past, or the experience you expect to pass through in the future. Such a practice will scatter your forces and divide your attention. The result will be confused mental action, to be followed by confused nervous action. This practice will also decrease your power of concentration; and without concentration we can accomplish nothing. The peaceful contemplation, however, of past joys or expected future joys, will produce nothing but good effects, provided we do nothing else while we indulge in such contemplation. In fact, to give special moments to such contemplation every day will prove beneficial. It matters not what we may be thinking about during our spare moments whether it be the past, the present, or the future so the thought is pleasant and attention is undivided.

To prevent completely, or permanently cure, nervousness, therefore, we should always bear these two things in mind: To avoid divided attention and to avoid the energy of the system running low. In other words, so live and think that your system will be brimful of energy at all times, and give your whole attention now to whatever you may be thinking of or doing now.

THE following exercises or methods may be employed most profitably, both in the prevention and in the cure of nervousness; and where faithful application is continued, the most perfect results will positively be secured: Place yourself in a calm attitude for a few minutes several times every day. See how quiet you can be in mind and body during those moments, and see how fully you can realize the deep stillness of your entire nature. By making it a practice to be deeply quiet for a few minutes several times a day, you can check completely any tendency toward nervousness. Besides, those moments will serve to recuperate your system, and you can do more and better work during any given period of time. During those quiet moments, relax mind and body completely. Let go of every muscle and every thought. Just be still, and think only of how delightful it feels to be perfectly still.

Aim to increase and deepen your consciousness of harmony. Think of the real meaning of harmony at frequent intervals, and try to inwardly feel that real harmony. In other words, make it a practice to turn your attention upon the idea of harmony itself, with a view of getting your system into the very life or soul of perfect harmony. You will soon begin to feel more harmonious, because we always tend to develop in ourselves every state or condition to which we give constant thought and attention. Mentally see yourself calm. Whenever you think of yourself, think of yourself as being calm, masterful and self-possessed. Every mental picture that you may form of yourself should appear in the attitude of calmness, and whenever you think of yourself as being in any position in which you expect to be placed, picture yourself as being calm and poised while in that position. You thus produce a tendency toward calmness, and you are daily becoming more and more serene and self-possessed until you place yourself in that masterful attitude that is both deeply peaceful and immensely strong.

Whenever you feel deeply, proceed at once to feel peaceful. You thus impress peace, harmony and calmness upon the subconscious mind; and the more you impress peace upon the subconscious the more peaceful you will feel throughout your interior nature. The undercurrents of your life will become harmonious and serene in their actions. You will feel peaceful and calm on the inside, in the depths of your real life and thought; and it is the man who feels calm and serene in the depths of his interior nature who also feels the greater power of his interior nature. Such a man is strong and masterful. Such a man has real will power.

Such a man has full possession of himself all that is in himself; and he has not only gained the power to be well, but the power to do things worthwhile. Always remember the great law: The deeper your consciousness of peace the greater your possession of power.

Refuse to be sensitive. Never say that you are sensitive. Never think that you are sensitive. When you are on the verge of feeling hurt, say to yourself that you can stand anything, and resolve to make good in that respect. Refuse to be offended at anything. Refuse to stoop to the petty position of being insulted, and refuse to accept any form of indignity that may be intended for you. Have too much respect for your nervous system to feel badly about anything that may be said or done, and have too much good sense to waste energy brooding over troubles when you know that that same energy, if put to good use, could put all your troubles to flight.

Never dwell mentally on anything that is unpleasant. To do so is to rob your nervous system of its very life. To brood over misfortune, trouble or loss is to steal energy and life from the nerves and organs of your body for no other purpose than to keep alive the ugly and distressing memories that those misfortunes have impressed upon your mind. When you do this, you are simply starving your nervous system in order that you may perpetuate the existence of mental monsters. The result will be nervousness, then nervous breakdowns, and in many instances the loss of mind or life. But all of this can easily be prevented. Refuse absolutely to remember the unpleasantness of the past or dwell on the dark side of anything that may exist in the present. Turn your attention at once to the richer and greater possibilities that every experience may contain, and enter positively into the very spirit of those possibilities. You will soon realize that your gain is greater than your loss, and that you have the power in the coming days to multiply this gain any number of times.

Never think of nerves. Never say that you are nervous, and never give conscious thought to any condition that may exist anywhere in your system. When you feel that something is wrong proceed to make it right, and the less you think of the wrong, or the organ in which the wrong may exist, the better. Think of your entire body as being wholesome all the way through, and live constantly in the life, the health and the strength of that thought. When you wish to change physical conditions, do not act mentally upon the physical body, and do not concentrate attention upon physical organs. The course to pursue is to produce the desired cause in the subconscious mind, and the desired effect will shortly appear in the physical personality. Do not permit for a moment any form of the high-strung attitude of mind. If you are addicted to this habit or tendency, cultivate relaxed calmness by frequently letting your whole system go into the feeling of deep calmness. To accomplish this, try to picture the inner world of deep calmness in which you live, and move, and have your being. Then simply let yourself go into the serene life and deeper soul calmness of this world. Also employ the special method given in the first part of this lesson whenever your nerves are on the verge of being strung up. That method will invariably produce relaxation, and besides, is quieting, soothing and recuperative to an exceptional degree.

Cultivate poise, wholesome mental states, and be deeply joyous at all times; but let your joy be of that nature that tends to produce a peaceful contentment. Avoid joyous attitudes that tend to excite the nerves, or that may produce an overwrought condition of mind. It is the deep, calm happiness, the happiness that becomes deeper and sweeter, as well as more peaceful, the longer it is enjoyed, that we should seek under every circumstance. This form of happiness cure should be taken every hour. Then be at peace with all things. Take plenty of sleep, and live in faith that all things are working together for greater and greater good.

2. Good Health for the Mind

TO secure and maintain perfect health and wholeness of mind, these important facts should be carefully considered:

1. In the prevention and cure of ailments that are almost wholly mental in their nature, there are two tendencies in particular that must be avoided, and these are the tendency to deplete the energies of the mind through the wrong use of mental action, and the tendency to intensify, under certain strained circumstances, the actions of those energies.

2. When the life and the energy of the mind is weakened to a point where there is not enough power to carry on normal thinking, the mind ceases to a degree to function according to its true nature, consciousness becomes so dull that no experience is correctly interpreted, and those mental conceptions that are formed at the time are mostly illusions. It requires energy to think and know, just the same as it requires energy to walk or move

physically. When the body loses too much energy it becomes too weak to walk; and when the mind loses too much energy it becomes too weak to think. But inability to walk is not always produced by a lack of physical energy; nor is inability to think clearly always produced by mental weakness.

3. The mind may be full of power, but when that power is abnormally intensified we find that harmonious and consecutive mental actions are interfered with, and clear thinking becomes impossible. Such a mind usually thinks a good deal, and is constantly in a worked-up condition; but the thinking will be disconnected, and false beliefs and ideas, and even hallucinations of every description, may result.

4. A close study of those ills that are mental in their nature proves clearly that when overworked conditions and worked-up conditions are avoided the mind will never become abnormal, unbalanced or disturbed. Overworked conditions,

however, do not come solely from too much mental exertion; but may also come from worry, depression, grief, fear, anxiety, and the like. These states of mind deplete the mental forces by using up energy in destructive thinking, while ordinary mental work consumes energy in performing what may be useful. Occasionally a person may work the mind so hard that too much energy is consumed, and we may have in such cases mental troubles coming directly from overwork. But such cases are very rare, as by far the greater number comes from worry and anxiety. An hour's worry will use up more mental energy than ten hours of steady brain work; and the same is true of fear, grief, depression and similar wrong mental states. It is usually the worry that goes with the work that makes a person feel exhausted after the work; and there are few who do not worry about something while at work; but this is a habit that not only can be but should be overcome completely.

5. When a person studies he imagines that hard study is wearing on the mind, and accordingly the mind is used up more or less during such work ; but he is mistaken in his idea. Study will use up a certain amount of mental energy, but not enough, even after many hours of continued study, to produce mental weariness. It is the anxiety that most students combine with their study that wears on the mind. When study is taken up for a certain purpose, the student is usually over-anxious to fulfill that purpose, and frequently there is fear lest failure should come, or depression on account of mistakes that already have been made. All of these misuses of the mind exhaust the mind so that the study cannot be carried out with satisfaction, while the study itself hardly ever exhausts or wearies the mind.

6. To prevent the mind from becoming weak we should establish faith in the place of worry, fear and anxiety. That mind that dwells, thinks and works in faith will always be strong. This is one of those great truths

that we should always remember; and to live in that truth is to provide the mind with a protection that has no equal.

7. Worked-up conditions of mind come principally from anger, excitement, intense action of mind or body, or from nervous rush; though any forceful mental action or any strained action will produce the same condition. In this condition the mind is strung up, so to speak, and throws its energies out of their normal spheres. They are therefore misdirected and finally lost, but on their way to complete loss they usually produce all sorts of illusions, and this accounts for the fact that a mind that is out of harmony with itself usually produces illusions along several lines without being conscious of doing so.

8. When the mind dwells too much on one isolated subject, or is forced too long in one direction, a similar condition is produced, and mental equilibrium is lost. In this condition one part of the mind will be overworked, while the other parts will

become practically dormant. The overworked part, therefore, will be unable to think clearly on account of its exhausted or intensified condition, while the dormant parts will be unable to think clearly on account of their state of inactivity. The result will be that the various states of mind produced at the time will be wrong, and wrong states invariably lead to ill health, both of mind and body.

9. To avoid the tendency to apply the mind too much in any one direction, every one should make it a habit to engage in what may be called mental variety; that is, there should be change of mental action, mental work, and interest at frequent intervals. This practice is most important when the system is more or less in nervous conditions. During such conditions sensitiveness is very keen, and every deeply-formed impression will tend to carry the mind away along any line that may be indicated by that impression. At such times, therefore, the tendency to cause the mind to act in one

direction only is very marked, and should be avoided completely at the very outset. Whenever a tendency is felt to move in any one mental direction exclusively, attention should be turned at once upon something else, so as to call into action the other parts of the mind, as the mind will usually return to wholesome action when every part of it becomes active. It is a splendid practice, in this connection, to study all kinds of subjects that have worth, in addition to what may engage one's attention in his vocation, and also to exercise all the functions of body, mind and soul as completely and harmoniously as possible.

10. All forms of fanaticism and prolonged actions of enthusiasm must be avoided completely, and no part of the mind should be permitted to run in a groove. It is a well-known fact that whenever anyone begins to become a fanatic, his mind becomes more or less unbalanced, and he becomes unable to see more than one side of any subject that he may consider. When this condition is

prolonged it leads to intense mental action along a single line, which will finally produce the conditions just mentioned. A fanatical mind is never a healthy mind, and is wrong on nearly all subjects, as well as being unwholesome in most of its usual mental states. As soon as a tendency to isolate action of mind is discovered in any part of thought or thinking, a new experience should be sought at once; and when we find ourselves completely absorbed in certain places, persons or things, we should immediately proceed to look for superior qualities in other things.

11. To prevent worked-up or overwrought conditions of mind it is necessary to cultivate perfect poise. All, therefore, who have a tendency to use the mind in such ways should proceed at once to acquire poise. In a few minutes, or even in much less time, the normal action of mind and body will be restored perfectly, and a great deal of energy will be added both to physical and mental action.

12. The mind must never permit itself to go down into any of the depressed states of feeling, as such a tendency invariably leads to mental ill health. To overcome this tendency, a sunny disposition should be cultivated, and the habit of fixing attention on the larger, the better, the superior, and the ideal in all things should be made a permanent factor in all lines of thinking. The fact that cheerfulness and ascending attitudes of mind add a great deal of power both to mind and body, is important; and it is well to remember in this connection that a cheerful, optimistic, ascending state of mind can be made so strong that no experience we may encounter can possibly make us depressed or discouraged. In connection with this phase of the study we shall find it profitable to refer to what was stated on mental tendencies in a previous lesson.

13. The importance of avoiding the downward tendency of the mind will be realized when we understand that all

depressing conditions invariably take the mind down nearer to that point where clear thinking becomes impossible; and, conversely, that all ascending or elevating attitudes of mind invariably cause the mind to act in those higher and clearer realms of thinking where all thinking functions, so to speak, in a world of mental light. In other words, the higher the mind ascends in conscious action the more light it will receive on any thought, and the clearer will all thinking become, accordingly.

14. To eliminate adverse conditions of the mind the first essential is to become mentally quiet, and the second essential is to provide more life and energy for the entire nervous system. To make the mind quiet the special method given for nervousness in the preceding lesson should be employed; and to provide more life and energy for the mind and nervous system, the various energies of the mind should be re-directed so that they may proceed along new lines. When the energies of the mind proceed along new

lines they will call into action other parts of the mind, and consequently bring forth the dormant mental power. The full power of the mind will thereby be restored in a short time, and perfect health and wholeness of mind will invariably follow.

3. The Cure of Despondency

THE fields and the gardens in the without require sunshine before they can bring forth their richness and beauty, and it is the same with the gardens of the wonderful within. Recent discoveries in psychology have revealed the fact that no mental talent or faculty can grow to any satisfaction unless the mind realizes an abundance of brightness and joy. There must be sunshine in the mind if the mind is to develop, and so long as this mental sunshine is continuous, development will be continuous provided the mental soil is made rich through rich thought, and well cultivated by being and doing. Rich thought, however, is not out of the reach of the average mind, neither is the effort to be and to do lacking among the majority; but the art of living continuously in a world of mental sunshine that is something that is lacking almost everywhere. But it is a lack that must be supplied before we can become and achieve as we should.

To be happy is profitable. This is one of the new thoughts of the new age, and it will prove a great thought to all who receive it in the right frame of mind. To cultivate cheerfulness is just as necessary as to cultivate ability and skill. So, therefore, the prevention or cure of despondency is just as important as the prevention or cure of any physical disease. The despondent mind is a sick mind, and a sick mind is more of an obstacle to human welfare than a sick body. For this reason no one can afford to live on any other side than the sunny side. All other sides mean sickness, failure and premature death. If our object in life is progress, growth, advancement and perpetual increase we must eliminate despondency in all its phases, and permanently establish in its place a state of perpetual joy. Happiness is the normal state of mind. When your mind is in perfect health it is always happy. In fact, a healthy mind cannot be otherwise than happy. Therefore, when you are not happy your mind is sick and needs attention. And it needs attention, first, because a sick mind may produce both moral and physical disease; and second, because a sick mind cannot do its work properly. Thousands of cases of intemperance and crime can be traced to sick or disappointed minds. And tens of thousands of failures had their beginnings in the same way. To overcome despondency, therefore, and all phases of unhappiness is a matter of the greatest importance.

When we study the subject closely we find that there are two kinds of despondency, each one having its own causes and requiring its own special remedies. The first of these will require but little attention, as it can hardly be called a mental ailment, being rather a symptom of disordered thoughts and wrong viewpoints. It usually rises from unpleasant experience such as disappointments from failure or defeat, and is therefore easily removed by training the mind to count everything joy, and by resolving to go in to win, no matter what present conditions may indicate.

When we look at life from the higher viewpoint, from the viewpoint of the real greatness of man, we will lose neither hope nor courage though we fail repeatedly. From this viewpoint we discover that every failure can be made a stepping-stone to success, and we proceed to use failure in that way whenever it appears. If we are to use failure in this way, however, we must never permit ourselves to fall into despair, but must meet every occasion in the attitude of complete self-mastery. Every failure is simply valuable energy gone astray, and if we approach this misdirected energy in the right attitude we can regain its possession and cause it to work for our advantage.

Therefore, those forces in our present circumstances that may seem to be destructive can be changed and made constructive. The reason why is simple. If we can change the direction of our forces or circumstances by wrong action we can also change the direction of those forces through right action, and thus cause those forces to work according to our purpose and plan. In consequence, when failure comes we should not give up in despair, but should cheerfully and masterfully gather together the scattered forces and re-direct them toward the construction of greater success than we ever knew before. The man who knows that his possibilities are unlimited will never give up to defeat, and therefore will never become despondent. He knows that he will win sooner or later if he continues as he has begun. And he also knows that every great difficulty that he overcomes invariably means added power to the victor. Such a mind can never be disappointed even though he should lose and fail in many places. He knows that he has destiny in his own hands and must inevitably attain whatever he has in view.

When we understand metaphysical laws we know that we cannot afford to become disappointed at any time, no matter how wrong things may seem to go, for the fact is that if we continue to be cheerful, hopeful and full of faith we are in that attitude through which we can apply our powers and talents successfully in causing all things to go right. In consequence, the despondency that comes from failure or defeat can easily be overcome or prevented by looking at life from the higher point of view. When we know our own possibilities and are constantly learning more thoroughly how to master and control our fate we shall never mind a few reverses. They are but temporary, and under the hand of the mind that knows, will soon give way to order, advancement and greater achievement. We may therefore pass this form of despondency without further consideration, knowing that the mind who understands his powers will never get sad or depressed from defeat anymore.

THE second form of despondency is actually a mental disease, and must be dealt with as such. It is produced in various ways and at times comes from the conditions mentioned above. As a rule, however, it originates in other ways. People have chronic despondency who have everything that heart can wish for, and who never knew disappointment or defeat. Sometimes this form of despondency is called melancholy and is the principal cause of insanity. Here it is well to remember that no mind can ever become insane that is always happy a great truth that should be well considered and thoroughly applied under every circumstance.

The chief causes of chronic despondency are as follows: First, exhaustion of nerve force or mental vitality; second, the misdirection of the emotions; third, disturbance in the chief nerve centers, especially the solar plexus; and fourth, disordered physical activities. The first cause is easily prevented, and the conditions that arise from this cause can be removed through very simple methods. There is usually sufficient vitality generated in the human system to supply all requirements, and unless this vitality is misused there will be no exhaustion whatever of mind or body. But discord, worry, anger, fear and similar states of mind tend to waste vital energy and, consequently, may bring about exhaustion. Regular work, however, will never produce this condition, as it has been conclusively demonstrated that work alone never does exhaust the vital forces of the human system. Despondency from exhausted vitality comes suddenly as a rule, and even when everything in your life seems conducive to harmony and joy. Under such circumstances the experience is mysterious. You can find no definite cause. Everything seems all right in your world, but you feel all wrong, and the conditions may last for hours. The temptation to seek remedies among stimulants is very strong at such times, and it is a well-known fact that nervous exhaustion has been the original cause of many a life gone wrong through the liquor habit. Instead of seeking artificial remedies, however, we should look for the cause and try to remove it directly.

When you feel fagged out, so to speak, in mind or body, you may know that the cause is low vitality. The first step to take when you make this discovery is to practice deep, full breathing, as there is nothing that will increase the vital forces so readily as right breathing.

And by right breathing we mean breathing that is deep, full and gentle, the entire chest being employed in the exercise. The average person, however, employs only the upper half of the lungs while breathing, thereby making himself liable to ailments in that part of his body, as well as tending to reduce the regular supply of vital energy. The simple science of right breathing is to breathe with the entire chest and to make all breathing orderly. When you feel the vital energies of the system running low breathe more, and if you have the opportunity to be perfectly quiet for a few minutes, trying at the time to realize that you are the vital center about which all the forces in your world tend to accumulate. And this is true. You are a vital center of all the elements and forces in your world, and when you concentrate your attention upon yourself as a vital center of life, you begin to accumulate more life until you are actually filled with more energy than you ever felt before. To hold yourself in this attitude for a few moments is to re-charge your system, and instead of feeling depressed you will soon begin to feel happier and better than you have felt for a long time.

When concentrating upon yourself as a living center, hold yourself in perfect poise, realizing that you live and move and have your being in an infinite sea of life; then gently desire to accumulate all the energy you can appropriate and remain silent for a few minutes in that attitude.

The results will be far beyond your expectations. A number of despondent states are produced by misdirected emotions, and the chief cause of misdirected emotions is found in the practice of entertaining desires that cannot be realized at the present moment. When energies accumulate in certain parts of the human system, where they cannot be employed at the time, the effect is always disturbing and depressing upon the nervous system, which in turn produces mental despondency; in other words, whenever unused forces accumulate anywhere they tend to aggravate the nerves in that region of mind or body, and this disturbance perverts the feelings and the emotions. So long as there is a strong tendency to express energy of any kind in any direction, a great deal of energy will move in that direction, and if it is denied expression it will accumulate, and this accumulation will produce abnormal conditions in that part of mind or body, the reaction of which always produces a disagreeable feeling in mind. To prevent this we must learn to entertain only such desires as can be realized at the present time, and also learn how to transmute our energies so that all that energy that cannot be employed in certain functions at the time may be drawn into other functions where more energy can be used to advantage. We should never permit the existence of a desire that cannot be realized at the time. When such desires arise we should turn our attention at once to something else. This turning of attention will tend to draw the energy connected with that desire toward other parts of the system where practical use can be realized.

In this connection a few illustrations will be found valuable. If you cannot honestly satisfy your desire for elegant clothes, change that desire and desire a beautiful soul instead. If you cannot afford to satisfy your desire for rich food, train yourself to desire rich thoughts instead. If you cannot at present satisfy your desire for physical progeny, turn your attention upon the mind and create great talent instead. Any number of similar illustrations can be given to bring out the idea intended, and all who will apply this idea will find it an easy matter to prevent all this physical and mental disturbance that may arise in the system when our energies are not permitted to express themselves along the original channels.

In gaining more perfect control over the energies of our system so that we can apply them whenever we may like, we should proceed in the realization of the fact that all energy, whether physical or mental, can be drawn into any organ, any function, or any faculty where we may need extra energy at the time; and as that realization becomes strong and vivid we shall find that a mere desire to cause our energy to accumulate in any particular part of mind or body where present action is taking place will cause all the surplus energy of the system to flow directly toward that place without delay.

ANOTHER cause of misdirected emotion is found in uncontrolled feelings. When we permit our feelings of joy to become what may be called hysterical ecstasy or permit our enthusiasm to take us off from our feet, we are preparing the way for a great fall of the mind. Despondency will follow. Every feeling and every joy must be held in poise, and enthusiasm has its greatest power when perfectly controlled. That form of enthusiasm that runs away from people invariably produces abnormal states of mind, and this is one thing we must do our best to avoid. Whenever a certain emotional state through lack of control goes so far in a certain direction that it usurps the whole attention of mind, more energy will accumulate in that place than can be used. This accumulation will depress the mind because it becomes a burden, while those other parts of mentality that have been depleted will experience a feeling of emptiness; and here you find the reason why you feel as if you had neither force, ability, nor ambition whenever you feel depressed.

When we are never overjoyed nor overenthused, when we never permit the existence of desires that can never be satisfied, and when we never permit any feeling to go beyond our control, we shall prevent entirely all depression that may arise from the misuse of emotions. But should despondency come from any source whatever we can remedy the matter in a few minutes by concentrating attention upon the brain center as outlined in the remedy for nervousness in a previous lesson, proceeding at the time to practice deep and full breathing. Through these methods we shall restore the equilibrium in the nervous system and at the same time increase the vital energy all through the system.

When we come to consider those forms of despondency that arise from a disturbed solar plexus we are face to face with a problem that sometimes appears to be mysterious, the reason being that the solar plexus is considered by many to be the connecting link between the physical and the metaphysical sides of the human system.

Those who accept this idea naturally believe that a great deal of extra energy would be liberated if the solar plexus were made more active, but this is not true. The fact is that the less conscious attention we give to the solar plexus the better. Disturbances that arise in the solar plexus invariably come from imperfect digestion, and when the solar plexus is disturbed it tends invariably to disturb all our feelings, both physical and mental. We find, therefore, that despondency coming in this way has its original cause in an imperfect digestion.

For this reason we shall find that some of the most severe cases of despondency are not premonitions of terrible disasters near at hand, as many people sometimes think; but have no other source than the stomach. In fact, it can be safely stated that more than three-fourths of the cases of despondency have their origin in a poor digestion. A good digestion, therefore, especially if reinforced with a well-poised harmonious nervous system, will prevent the larger part of the despondency that may come to the average individual. And knowing this, we realize the folly of taking despondency with so much seriousness. If we would make it a practice instead to look upon those conditions as of no particular moment, and then proceed to place our digestion in order, we should go very far toward restoring mental health and wholeness for all time.

Those cases of despondency that come from physical disturbance are found only among people who have strong psychical tendencies, but who do not know how to use those new forces that have arisen in their deeper mental life. Whenever a new power is awakened the knowledge of how to use it should be at hand, and there will be no serious mistakes in this application. This being true, no one should attempt to use a new power, whatever it may be, until well informed as to its nature and right use. That form of despondency, however, that comes through psychical disturbance is usually of a serious nature, and everything possible should be done to prevent it completely. To prevent this condition there is but one safe course to follow, and that is to have nothing whatever to do with psychical phenomena or psychical experience until you understand fully the psychological and metaphysical laws that underlie the phenomena, or until you have attained perfect mastery over yourself. To a great many minds, however, these requirements may seem too stringent. In fact, if one should comply with these requirements it would be impossible for anyone to engage in psychical research; and though this is practically true, it is also true that most of us will find it greatly to our advantage to give no attention to psychical research whatever. The subject of despondency, however, is one that should receive our best attention, and every method that we can find, in addition to those presented above, should be employed if such methods will remove the tendency of the mind to become depressed. We know that the growing mind as well as the healthy mind needs continuous sunshine, and knowing this we shall certainly do our best to provide this sunshine under every circumstance. Our object is not only health, but the power to do greater things in the world. And as the realization of both of these objects demands a growing mind, we shall find it most profitable to provide that mental sunshine that can cause mental growth to be continuous.

4. The Prevention of Mental Depression

IN addition to what has been said on this subject in preceding pages, we find two special causes that frequently result in chronic mental depression. The first cause is found in the presence of certain adverse mental states that have become so deep-seated that they affect the subconscious life, and the second cause is found in the presence of awakened subconscious forces that cannot find a full and natural expression.

There is many a person who is suffering from mental depression simply because the genius within him is trying to force itself out in tangible action, but cannot produce such action on account of the inharmony existing between the objective and the subjective states of mind. When there is a great deal of power within that wants to act, but cannot find an opportunity to act, an unnatural pressure will be produced in various parts of the mentality, and mental depression will usually result. This depression, involving more or less gloom, disappointment and even despair, may continue for years, and this accounts for the fact that there is many a genius, or possible genius, who is unhappy almost constantly. The outer mind of the average person has not been trained to respond to the power and the genius of the subconscious. Therefore, the genius within is held in prison, so to speak. It is not permitted to come out and act. It is confined behind the bars of objective limitations and refuses to reconcile itself to such a fate. In some minds the power within, not being very active, is seldom felt, while in others the powers of the great within are constantly clamoring for freedom and expression. It is this that produces unrest, dissatisfaction, mental depression and that seemingly hopeless longing for the ideal that sensitive minds find so difficult to bear. When the objective mind is placed in such a complete harmony with the subconscious that the power of the within can come forth and do what it wants to do, we have the peace that passes understanding, the harmony that touches the very ecstasy of the soul, and the joy that cannot be measured. At such moments the individual is in the now, all that he can be in the now, and his life is complete. But such moments come rarely to the average person, the reason being that his outer mind is not in a condition to give expression to the life and the power that is being awakened in the great within.

The average person is not trained to give expression to the genius from within. It is simply trained to remember what others have said and to imitate what others have done. In the meantime the genius within is held in prison, and in trying to gain freedom produces much confusion, much depression, many mistakes and many moments of mental despair. A great deal of the unhappiness that comes to most ambitious people originates in these very conditions. The mental household is divided against itself. The inner mind wants to produce the greatness and the joy of the full individual life, while the outer mind wants to live a superficial life and do only what the senses in their limitations may desire to do. The objective mind, however, was not created to act at variance with the subconscious. It is generations of unscientific training that has given the outer mind this tendency, but there can be neither real peace nor real greatness in the mind of man until this tendency is removed.

The two minds must work together in harmony and for the same purpose. The objective mind should daily impress the subconscious with its highest thoughts, aims, desires, and should respond perfectly when the subconscious brings forth the power with which those aims and desires may be fulfilled. The objective mind should constantly expect more and more power from the subconscious, and should constantly hold itself in that calm, well-poised receptive attitude which is so necessary to the full expression of the greater power from within. To cultivate this attitude is to place the two minds in harmony, and as the objective mind is daily directing the subconscious to produce more life, greater intelligence and greater power, this harmony will enable the subconscious to come forth and do what it has been directed to do. The majority of those who suffer from mental depression, discontent, chronic despondency, or an inclination to live on the dark side of life will find complete emancipation from those conditions when the greater power within them has been given full freedom to act. To place the conscious and the subconscious in harmony is to give the entire power within an opportunity to express itself, and relief will come at once. In addition, the entire personality will be re-charged with new life, the body will become more vigorous, and the mind more brilliant.

When chronic mental depression comes from adverse mental states, the remedy is to train the objective mind in exact scientific thinking. That is, the mind should live on the sunny side, the constructive side, the growing side, and every thought should be formed in the exact likeness of the highest ideals that can be created. When we concentrate our attention upon our ideals, and deeply feel at all times that we are moving toward those ideals, we will proceed to rise out of depression, darkness and discontent into the world of light, freedom, peace and joy. There is an upper region in the mind of man where happiness is perpetual. To enter this upper region the first essential is to place the two minds in harmony, and the second essential is to keep the eye single upon the heights of all that is true, all that is perfect, all that is lofty, all that is beautiful, and all that is sublime.

5. How to Remove Fear

SO long as there is a tendency to fear it is not possible for any mind to do its best, and as it is absolutely necessary for every mind to do its best in order to live the life of peace, health, freedom, and attainment, we must proceed to remove fear completely. The real origin of all human ills can be traced to retarded growth, and we know that growth is retarded whenever we fail to do our best. Everything, therefore, that interferes with the being of our best must be removed; and there are many things that interfere in this manner, but the attitude of fear is one of the most pronounced. It is possible to demonstrate that fear has prevented more natural-born great minds from applying their greatness than all other adverse states of mind combined; and it is also possible to demonstrate that fear has produced more disease, trouble and misfortune than any other cause. To remove fear, therefore, would be doing something that would be extraordinary, to say the least.

There are many methods that will remove fear temporarily, but to remove it permanently we must find its fundamental cause. This cause has been sought far and wide, and has been found in what may be termed the outer time of the present moment. Reduced to its last analysis, fear is simply a state of mind arising from the seeming uncertainty of the immediate future. If we knew that everything in the coming days would be exactly as we wished it to be there would be no occasion for fear at any time; but it is in this uncertainty with which we come in mental contact nearly every day that gives origin to every form of fear. To remove fear, therefore, this state of uncertainty must be overcome; and it is good news to know that this is possible. This feeling of uncertainty gives origin to a number of forms of fear, and one of the most pronounced is possibly the fear of death. We fear death because we feel an uncertainty with regard to the life beyond; but if we positively knew that death was simply the open door to a larger and more wonderful world than this, the thought of death could never produce fear in the least.

Another phase is that of calamity. We live more or less in the dread of calamities, because we do not know whether we shall escape safely or not, nor do we always know what precaution to take that absolute safety may be secured.

We fear poverty because things in this world seem so uncertain. Our friends everywhere meet unexpected misfortune, and we imagine that the same fate is quite likely to come to us. If we could master our circumstances we should think differently about this particular phase; but the art of mastering circumstances is not clearly understood, consequently the majority continue to fear the possible misfortune of the future. We fear disease because we are almost daily brought face to face with threatening symptoms, and we see people all about us going down to the grave through the continued actions of what at first seemed to be but insignificant symptoms. There are scores of other conditions and things that we fear more or less, and for the same reason; that is, we are uncertain as to the outcome.

The outcome may be good or ill; we do not know, and we fear that it may be the latter, because we have not acquired the power to produce the former at will. It is therefore evident that all fear comes directly from uncertainty as to the immediate future, as to the results of what we are doing now. What is brewing in the present has frequently been brewing in the past, and in the past such indications have many times turned out badly; and the question is. Can we make everything come right this time? Most of us do not know, and that is the reason why the majority are almost in constant fear concerning the events of the near future.

That fear comes from uncertainty, and from no other cause, is easily demonstrated; but the question is what it is that produces this uncertainty. When we analyze that phase of the subject we find that the cause of every form of uncertainty is produced by the fact that similar things under similar adverse conditions turned out badly before, and we have nothing to prove at the present time that we can cause all things to come right in the future; that is, the majority have nothing to prove that the future can be made right, regardless of conditions in the present. Though the majority may not have this proof, that fact does not indicate that the proof cannot be found.

To remove fear it is therefore necessary to secure positive evidence to prove the idea that we can cause everything to come right, that we can make the future better than the present, and that we can cause all things to work together for the promotion of our highest welfare. The majority, however, may believe that such evidence cannot be secured, because they judge according to appearances and think of human nature as weak and incompetent, even at its best.

But those who understand the great law of cause and effect, and understand the real power of man, know that appearances do not reveal the exact truth concerning anything, and they also know that man has it in his power to change his whole life, his entire nature and his own destiny. This world is not a world of aimless chance; neither do events just happen. When we look at the confused surface and see how many things move in some helter-skelter fashion we may think that it is entirely useless to attempt any orderly readjustment ; but when we discover that every adverse effect comes from some adverse cause, and that man himself produces those adverse causes, we find it necessary to take another point of view.

The confused surface of the world is produced by the confused and misdirected actions of the human race, just as an upset household is produced by disorder among its members. The inside of every house is the exact likeness of those who have charge of it.

An orderly person will have everything in harmony, and neatness will prevail even though the house itself be ordinary, and everything in it be ordinary and inexpensive. But the newest and finest house and the costliest furniture can give the appearance of utter depravity if placed in charge of a disorderly mind.

The same law rules everywhere among the smallest things and the largest things in the world. The world itself and its many parts are like the people that are in charge. The good things in the world come from good causes; the other things come from adverse causes; and all causes come from man. Man, however, can produce any cause he likes; therefore the future is in his own hands.

To change the condition of the world in general, the human race in general must be changed, and this is possible. For a long period of time the race has been told to be right and good, but we have not been told clearly how to proceed. The race is most willing to change for the better; in fact, the great majority are constantly praying for the required knowledge and truth on the great subject of human betterment. All that is necessary, therefore, is to provide this greatly desired information which is already at hand, and the world will begin to change.

The world in general is the direct effect of the actions of all its people, while the world of the individual is the result of his own actions plus those actions of the general world with which he may come in contact. But he can change his own actions and also adapt himself to the actions of the world in such a way that the very results he desires can be secured in each instance. In other words, each individual can produce in his own world what he may desire; and he can so change those things that come into his world from the world in general, that they become identical in nature and action with what he himself is producing for himself.

To understand the real nature and the real power of man, is to know that he can determine what he himself is to produce, and that he can also determine what the world in general is to produce in his individual world. He is therefore complete master of the situation, and this being true, the entire subject is reduced to that of pure mathematics. When we are working out a problem in mathematics we do not dread the answer; if we know the principles, we have no fear as to the outcome. If we are good mathematicians we know positively that the answer will be correct, and there can be no fear or dread where one positively knows. The good mathematician, however, is not free from fear in his calculations because he is superior to others; he is superior only in this respect that he knows the principles involved. He lives in the same mathematical world as does the stumbling student.

The two are not different in kind. The only difference is that the one understands the principles and the other one does not. The good mathematician gets the answer he wants; he makes the future of the problem just what he wishes it to be. He wants the outcome to be right, and understanding the principles, he gets what he wants.

His simple secret is this: He knows what principles to apply in solving the problem, and he applies those principles in every problem. Accordingly, he gets the results desired. The problems we meet in every-day life can be dealt with in the same manner. They all have a mathematical basis, and if we apply the principles of life correctly those problems can be worked out so as to produce the right results in every case.

WHEN we know that the future is the direct outcome of the present there can be no fear concerning the future so long as we correctly apply the principles of life to everything that we may be doing in the present. Then we should remember, in addition, that the man who is living constructively every day is building for himself a future that is larger and better and more perfect than his present. He is positively convinced that the outcome of his present efforts will be good, and will produce the greater, because he knows that he is daily placing in action causes that are productive of better and greater things.

That such a man can have fear is simply impossible. There is no uncertainty in his mind, therefore there can be no fear in his mind. He has no fear of poverty, because he is daily improving himself, daily rendering better service to the world; and it is invariably the law that the better our service the better our recompense. There may be occasional exceptions to this rule, but these exceptions are seeming, and are due to certain violations of the laws of life that we do not happen to see at the time.

There are many who may be using certain principles correctly and misusing other principles. The results in those cases will therefore be uncertain, and fear may arise; but when we apply all the principles there can be no uncertainty and no fear, because the result will be as we desire. That man who has ability, and who properly relates himself to the needs of that sphere through which his ability may be fully expressed, will be in constant demand, and his recompense will steadily increase. When great minds are not appreciated in their own time, they themselves are to blame, the fault being that they do not adapt their genius to the needs of their own times. Anyone, however, no matter what his ability may be, can adapt himself to the needs of his own day, and thus not only receive full appreciation from his own generation, but fully apply in the most successful manner all the ability he may possess.

Those minds that are doing their best today have no occasion to fear provided the law is understood, because so long as they are doing their best they are becoming better, and will advance steadily. To such minds the future is bright. They are daily creating good causes, and the future will be more and more abundantly supplied with good effects. This is the law, therefore he who applies this law has nothing to fear.

To this statement everyone will agree; but with the average mind the problem is how to create good causes, and good causes only, and how to know whether or not living is constructive. There are thousands who mean well, and who are actually trying to create only the best, but they are living almost constantly in trouble and misfortune. The cause of this condition is found in the fact that they have not been taught how to apply the principles involved in those particular problems that come up in their lives.

To proceed, we must bring our life out of this chaotic condition and establish absolute order. Then upon this orderly foundation, no matter how small or insignificant it may be, we must begin the construction of a new mansion of life. Before we begin, however, the plans of the new structure must be clearly fixed in mind; that is, we must form our ideal. The first essential is to live in the peaceful, serene, well-poised attitude of mind, because the forces of life must be brought into the harmony of constructive action.

The second essential is to take life into our own hands by constantly holding life in the consciousness of our own possession; that is, we should always think of life as being absolutely in our own possession, and before long the power to completely govern our own life will become second nature. The third essential is to have one predominant purpose, that is, to make yourself and your work better and better every day, to build constantly for greater things both in your own nature and in your own environment. In this connection we must learn to see all things in our imagination as being made more and more perfect, because to keep ':he mental eye single upon the better side, the strong side and the superior side of everything, is to give the creative forces of mind a superior model; and these forces always create in the exact likeness of the model. When we think constantly of the superior, and keep the mental eye single upon the superior, we therefore create the superior in our own natures.

On the other hand, when we think of the dark side, the weak side, the troubled side, the sick side, and the failing side, we tend to create all those conditions in our nature and in our world; and when we fear we always think of those inferior sides, thereby causing that which we fear to come upon us.

When we concentrate our whole attention upon the construction of a superior life, and work with a constantly increasing knowledge of the art of using all our faculties constructively, we shall bring the whole of life into a perfect system of action, wherein all things will co-operate in producing for us the greater, the better and the superior. When all our energies are organized into an army of skilled builders there is only one effect possible, and that is the perpetual increase of everything that is desirable in human life. He who employs all his energies in this manner will therefore have nothing to fear, as in his life the very cause of fear will have been removed completely. It is therefore evident that the problem of removing fear is solved through the art of using all our faculties and forces in such a manner as to build more nobly in the present than we did in the past, and this we may accomplish by learning to use the principles of life with mathematical precision. There are many things that we are afraid of, but the principal ones are undoubtedly poverty, disease, calamity and death; and when we learn how to remove the fear of these four we shall also be able to remove the fear of all minor conditions that are not desired. To remove the fear of death it is only necessary to become convinced of the fact that life is continuous, and that the future life of each individual is the natural outcome of his present life.

The development of what may be termed the consciousness of soul, or the realization of the I Am and the perfection of the I Am, will demonstrate conclusively to any mind that the life of every individual is continuous and endless; in fact, to become conscious of the I Am is to know that the I Am and life are identical, and we know that life is indestructible. Then add to this the great fact that you, the real you, constitutes the I Am, and you have an exact basis upon which you may demonstrate to yourself through pure reason that you shall continue perpetually to live, THE understanding of the laws of cause and effect will demonstrate that you can create your own future and your own destiny, not only in the present sphere, but in future spheres of existence, and that you can make your future existence as beautiful, as marvelous and as gorgeous as your imagination can possibly picture. The law is, that he who is living nobly in the present is creating for himself a better future, both in this life and in the life to come; therefore he who applies the principles of that law, which simply mean the principles of right living and right thinking, has nothing to fear, neither from death nor from the future. In fact, death to him will simply mean the gates ajar to a far richer, far better and far more beautiful world than this; and the future to him will mean attainments, achievements and enjoyments so far superior to what anyone has realized in this world that words cannot possibly describe them.

In this connection it is interesting to know that they who have no fear of death always live the longest lives, the best lives and the happiest lives upon earth ; and it is also a well-known fact that they who know they are doing their best in the present are not afraid to leave this planet at any time. They dread no change, because they know that every change must be a change for the better. These people have inner conviction based upon the fact that they are applying principle in their lives; that it always will be well with those who do well; and we know that such a conviction will remove fear completely. When we learn how to live we shall lose all fear of death, because when we begin to actually live we know that we shall live a very long life, a very interesting life and a very beautiful life; and we also know that what is called death is but an open door to a still more beautiful life more beautiful because a beautiful present invariably produces a more beautiful future.

What we have earned, that we shall receive and enjoy. This is the law, and therefore he who so lives that he earns much, will have much to receive and enjoy in days to come.

When symptoms of disease appear, we know that we have violated some natural law; but if we understand life we also know that the pain is a good friend coming to inform us that something needs re-adjustment; and if we proceed to right the matter, which we can readily do when we know how to think and live, there will be no disease whatever. When we know how to remove all threatening symptoms at once we shall never fear disease; and when we know how to create health in greater and greater abundance, the fear of disease will become impossible. So long as we create health we cannot be sick; and every person who is living a constructive life who is applying the principles of life to his own living, as the mathematician applies principles to his problems is creating health in greater and greater abundance.

The fear of poverty will disappear when we learn that ability and power can be developed more and more for an indefinite period. We know that competent men and women are in great demand everywhere, and when we know that we can become competent sufficiently competent to fill the best places in the world we shall live in the assurance of perpetual increase, and all fear of poverty will therefore disappear. You cannot have any fear of poverty or loss when you know that your earning power is increasing every day, and that the demand for your services in the world is increasing every day.

To eliminate the fear of calamities, accidents, catastrophes and the like, may seem impossible because it is generally believed that the individual cannot control the causes through which those things are produced; but when we look closely at the matter we find that we meet those unpleasant events because we fail to do the right thing at the right time. When we live according to principles, we will learn more and more to do the right thing at the right time; and we shall also develop those finer senses as we grow in mind and soul, through which we can discern readily the course to pursue in each case, and thus avoid what might not prove agreeable. Then in this connection we should also remember that though we may not be able to control all the causes of calamities in the world, we can so well control ourselves that we can go out of the way of the actions of those causes. In other words, we can avoid the path that leads to calamity, and take those paths that are always safe.

When we apply the law of life in such a manner that we constantly create the better and the better, we shall positively meet more and more of the better. Accordingly, there will be nothing to fear, because as long as we create only the best we shall receive only the best in return.

THE END.

Printed in Great Britain
by Amazon